AMICUS ILLUSTRATED • AMICUS INK

DO YOU REALLY WANT TO MEET A SHARK?

WRITTEN BY CARI MEISTER   ILLUSTRATED BY DANIELE FABBRI

Amicus Illustrated and Amicus Ink
are imprints of Amicus
P.O. Box 1329
Mankato, MN 56002
www.amicuspublishing.us

Library of Congress Cataloging-in-Publication Data
Meister, Cari, author.
 Do you really want to meet a shark? / by Cari
Meister ; illustrated by Daniele Fabbri.
    pages cm. — (Do you really want to meet...?)
 Summary: "A child learns about several shark species
and then goes on a cage diving adventure to meet a
great white shark"— Provided by publisher.
 Audience: K to grade 3.
 ISBN 978-1-60753-737-3 (library binding)
 ISBN 978-1-60753-841-7 (ebook)
 ISBN 978-1-68152-011-7 (paperback)
 1. White shark—Juvenile literature. 2. Sharks—
Juvenile literature. I. Fabbri, Daniele, 1978- illustrator.
II. Title.
 QL638.95.L3M45 2016
 597.3'3—dc23   2014036519

Editor   Rebecca Glaser
Designer   Kathleen Petelinsek

Printed in the United States of America at
Corporate Graphics in North Mankato, Minnesota.

HC 10 9 8 7 6 5 4 3 2 1
PB 10 9 8 7 6 5 4 3 2 1

ABOUT THE AUTHOR

Cari Meister is the author of more than 120 books for children, including the *Tiny* (Penguin Books for Young Readers) series and *Snow White and the Seven Dogs* (Scholastic, 2014). She lives in Evergreen, Colorado, with her husband John, four sons, one horse, and one dog. You can visit Cari online at *www.carimeister.com*.

ABOUT THE ILLUSTRATOR

Daniele Fabbri was born in Ravenna, Italy, in 1978. He graduated from Istituto Europeo di Design in Milan, Italy, and started his career as a cartoon animator, storyboarder, and background designer for animated series. He has worked as a freelance illustrator since 2003, collaborating with international publishers and advertising agencies.

You say you want to meet a shark—one of the biggest predators in the sea. But did you know that around the world, there are more than 50 shark attacks on people every year?

Luckily, few people die from shark attacks. If a shark attacks you, you may live, but you may be missing an arm or leg. Once a shark bites off part of your body, he will NOT return it.

Do you REALLY want to meet a shark?

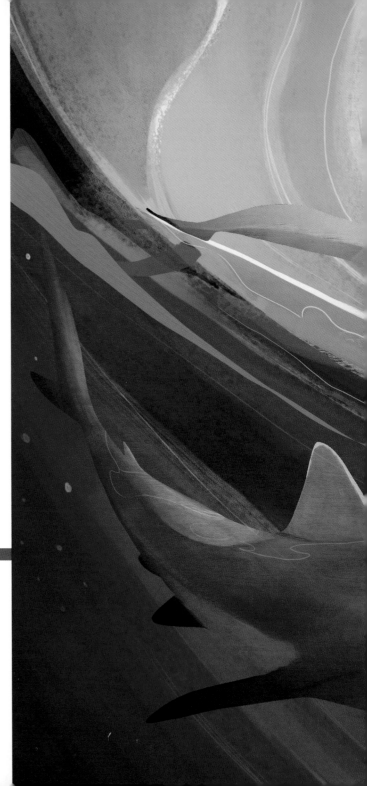

Okay, where do you want to go?
Sharks live all around the world.
Not all of them are dangerous.

The smallest shark is only the size of an adult's hand. It's called the Dwarf Lantern Shark. It lives off the northern coast of South America.

The largest shark—the whale shark—is about the size of a bus. It has massive jaws and more than 300 rows of teeth. But don't worry. Its teeth are small and dull. It eats plankton and small fish. Whale sharks live in all tropical oceans.

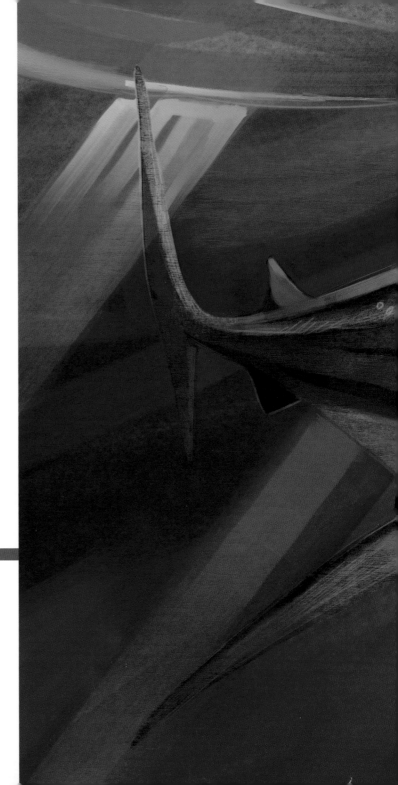

What's that? You want to meet a great white shark? A great white is one of the biggest and deadliest sharks in the sea. They can grow to be more than 20 feet (6m) long.

You want to meet one anyway? Okay, grab your wetsuit—you're off to California.

You finished your diving training, right? You'll need it to go cage diving. Yes, that's right—cage diving. If you want to meet a great white face-to-face, the safest place for you is in a metal cage. Hop aboard! The expedition guide knows just where to go.

Look! Elephant seals—a great white's favorite meal!

Do you see that fin? It could be the dorsal fin of a
shark. Get out the binoculars. It looks like a . . .

. . . SHARK!

CHOMP! CHOMP!

Look at his teeth! They are sharp and jagged—perfect for ripping his meal into chunks. It may be gruesome, but it's the way of the wild.

It's almost time to get in the cage. Put on your diving mask.
The guide will hook up the air hose.

CLANK! You're locked in. There's no turning back now.
Splash!

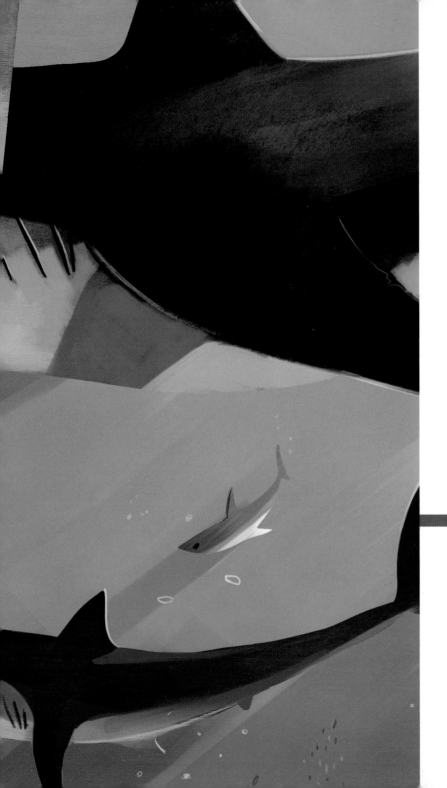

Incredible! Now you've REALLY
met a shark face-to-face!

WHERE DO SHARKS LIVE?

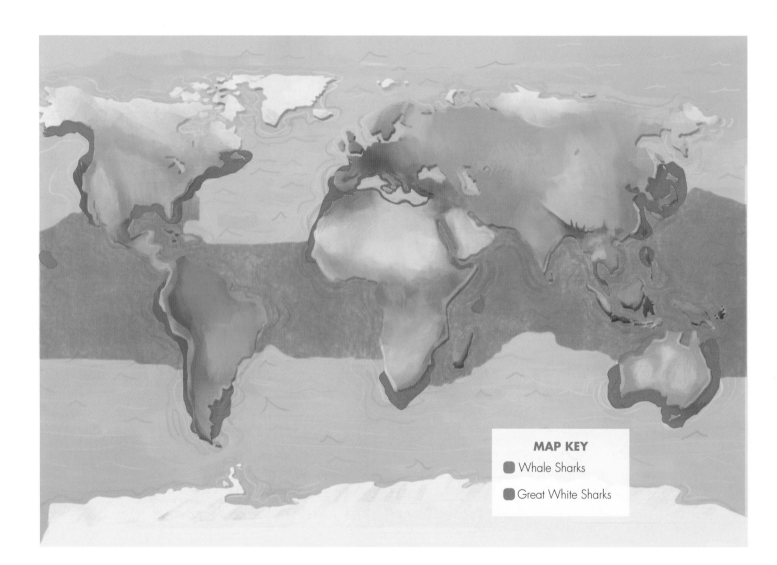

MAP KEY
- Whale Sharks
- Great White Sharks

GLOSSARY

cage diving When you go into a metal cage to look at sea animals in the wild.

dorsal fin A triangular fin on a shark's back that helps it balance in the water.

expedition A journey to go look for something, especially animals.

gruesome Disgusting or frightful.

massive Very large and heavy.

plankton Very small animals and plants that live in the ocean.

predator An animal that hunts other animals for food.

READ MORE

Green, Jen. **Great White Shark**. New York: Bearport, 2014.

Hibbert, Clare. **If You Were a Shark**. Mankato, Minn.: Smart Apple Media, 2014.

Roy, Katherine. Neighborhood Sharks: Hunting with the Great Whites of California's Farallon Islands. New York: David Macaulay Studio/Roaring Brook Press, 2014.

Turnbull, Stephanie. **Sharks**. Big Beasts. Mankato, Minn.: Smart Apple Media, 2015.

WEBSITES

Animal Fact Guide: Great White Shark
www.animalfactguide.com/animal-facts/great-white-shark
Read more about great white sharks.

National Geographic Kids: Great White Shark
kids.nationalgeographic.com/animals/great-white-shark.html
Research facts about great white sharks and compare its size to common objects.

Great White Video Clips—ARKive
www.arkive.org/great-white-shark/carcharodon-carcharias
Watch video clips of great whites in the ocean.

Sharks For Kids
sharks4kids.com
Learn about all kinds of sharks and shark anatomy, do fun games and activities, and learn what people are doing to protect sharks.

Every effort has been made to ensure that these websites are appropriate for children. However, because of the nature of the Internet, it is impossible to guarantee that these sites will remain active indefinitely or that their contents will not be altered.

DATE DUE

			PRINTED IN U.S.A.